Original title:
Leaves on the Edge

Copyright © 2025 Creative Arts Management OÜ
All rights reserved.

Author: Derek Caldwell
ISBN HARDBACK: 978-1-80581-765-9
ISBN PAPERBACK: 978-1-80581-292-0
ISBN EBOOK: 978-1-80581-765-9

Glimmers of Ephemeral Beauty

Tiny whispers fall and dance,
In a parade, they twirl and prance.
Caught in breezy, silly waltz,
Nature's jest, and none finds faults.

Round the corner, a squirrel's glee,
Chasing fortune like a spree.
With a skip and laugh so bold,
They snack on dreams, a sight to behold.

The Soft Kiss of Change

A mischief in the autumn air,
Tickles noses, catches hair.
Why do the trees wear coats of gold?
A fashion statement, truth be told.

Fluffy clouds take flight in glee,
Giggling at the old oak tree.
"Join the party!" they seem to shout,
While creatures frolic, twist, and pout.

Nature's Final Strokes

A final brush, the painter grins,
With silly swirls and dizzy spins.
Colors splash, then tumble down,
As laughter echoes all around.

The winds throw confetti all around,
As critters in chaos spin and bound.
"Who knew these shades would make us dance?"
In this folly, all take a chance.

Beauty in the Bluster

With every puff, the chaos reigns,
Nature's humor knows no chains.
Hats go flying, a comical scene,
As gusty giggles fill the green.

Trees bend low with chuckles bright,
"Join the frolic, what a sight!"
While over there, a cat meows,
"Do you see this? Just take a bow!"

Rustling Echoes Underfoot

The ground whispers secrets low,
Whimsical whispers, a comic show.
Tiny critters scurry about,
While old leaves giggle, there's no doubt.

Chasing shadows that flicker and dance,
They wiggle and wriggle in a prancy prance.
Branches chuckle, they crack a pun,
As autumn arrives, and summer's done.

A Tapestry of Transience

A patchwork quilt of colors bright,
Snickers from petals, a silly sight.
These playful hues in a swirling spin,
It's a nature's joke with a cheeky grin.

Skippers and flutterers join in the jest,
While nature replays its charming quest.
Dancing around, from tree to tree,
Laughter echoes, wild and free!

The Last Murmur of Green

The final titter of frolicsome tones,
Frogs in a chorus, making their loans.
Grinning grasshoppers hum a refrain,
While they tap-dance on puddles of rain.

A squirrel quips with a nutty remark,
As breezes toss branches, they leave a mark.
Stories ventured from roots beneath,
Chuckles abound; it's all in the wreath!

Ashes of Summer's Glory

The grand finale of summer's spree,
Whirling bits of comedy, just wait and see.
Dancing in circles, like a playful fight,
They tumble and rustle, a whimsical sight.

Sass from the twigs, a riotous cheer,
As winter creeps in, the end is near.
Yet in the fall's sigh, they play and jest,
With humor woven in autumn's best!

Where the Air Carries Secrets

In whispers soft, the breeze does brag,
A secret told by a sneaky rag.
The squirrels laugh in acorn attire,
While chatting mishaps they can't retire.

A chipmunk spins a yarn so tall,
About a bird that dared to crawl.
The wind just giggles, blowing swirls,
As nature's antics unfurl in twirls.

Ballet of the Desolate

In empty spaces, shadows dance,
With a broken twig that took a chance.
A clumsy thump, a skip, a slide,
The laughter stumbles, yet won't hide.

A bustling toad hops right on cue,
While crickets chirp a ditty or two.
The moon rolls her eyes, chuckling bright,
At this midnight ballet, a curious sight.

Threads of the Fading Year

As colors fade and skies have grown,
A spider weaves a tale all its own.
It catches jokes in a silken net,
Of autumn quirks, we won't forget.

The pumpkins grin, all orange and round,
As mischief brews just off the ground.
With each cold breeze, the giggles fly,
In threads of laughter low and high.

Chronicles of Twilight's Kiss

When dusk descends, the tales begin,
Of owls who gossip and raccoons that grin.
A firefly winks, storytellers unite,
In a sparkly argument, oh what a sight!

They plot and scheme with glee in the dark,
While bats perform, oh what a lark!
With moonbeams shining, oh, what a twist,
In the chronicles of a night not to miss.

Nature's Last Embrace

In a tree, a squirrel prances,
Dancing like it knew the chances.
But a gust came, oh so bold,
Sending him spiraling, uncontrolled.

Unruly leaves took flight with flair,
Tickling him as he swayed in air.
He swore they laughed, oh what a sight,
Nature's jesters, a pure delight!

Cradled in Twilight

The sun dips low, what a big show,
In a race with crickets, oh dear, who'll glow?
A wanderer trips, catching his breath,
Hoping dusk doesn't track his death.

A breeze whips past with playful glee,
Tugging at clothes, oh so cheekily.
He sweeps a branch, thinking it wise,
But a crow's cackle reveals the surprise!

Moments in the Drift

With every gust, the shadows prance,
   Like silly dancers in a chance.
A flip here, a flap there, oh so spry,
   Making a mockery as they fly.

A hollow log holds secrets tight,
While tiny bugs wiggle in fright.
They hide and seek in nature's game,
   Laughing silently, never the same.

The Edge of Whispered Dreams

Nighttime whispers on the breeze,
Tickling the branches with playful tease.
A raccoon sneaks, thinking it sly,
Until a branch snaps – oh my, oh my!

Moonlit pranks keep critters awake,
While shadows weave, no chance to shake.
A fruit bat hiccups mid-flight,
Delighting the owls with pure delight!

Memories Tucked in Boughs

Boughs are swaying, ducks do dance,
Squirrels giggle, take a chance.
In the breeze, stories twirl,
Nature's yuk-yuks, give a whirl.

Sunshine tickles, shadows play,
Laughter's echo, come what may.
Friendly whispers in the rust,
A branch's chuckle, it's a must!

When Stillness Prevails

Quiet moments, crickets sing,
Hats on cats, oh what a fling!
Sipping tea with a wiggly worm,
Jokes are overheard, they squirm.

Sitting still, the world's a show,
Even trees join in the flow.
Branches gossip, oh so sly,
As wind whispers a big ol' lie.

Echoing the Prairies

Prairies shout with giggles loud,
Hiccups echo, nature's crowd.
Cacti wear their prickly vests,
While tumbleweeds throw wild jests.

In this realm of silly sights,
Bouncing bunnies, playful flights.
A prairie dog, he skips and hops,
His boots squeak, the laughter stops!

The Final Breath of Color

A splash of red, a wink of gold,
Nature's exit, daring and bold.
Cracking jokes as shades retreat,
A final party, oh what a feat!

Wear your laughs like autumn's wear,
Dance with breezes, if you dare.
With each swirl, the giggles grow,
In this frolic, let's put on a show!

Echoes of Solitude and Sunshine

In the breeze, they dance and twirl,
A caper here, a silly swirl.
They wave goodbye, then wave back,
A merry troupe on a winding track.

With laughter caught in midair,
They gossip sweet without a care.
A jolly trail of giggles spread,
As shadows play with thoughts unsaid.

Crisp Whispers on the Ground

Crunchy sounds beneath my shoes,
A symphony of autumn's blues.
They crack and pop like popcorn treats,
A zany marching band in fleets.

From every twist, a chuckle grows,
As nature's humor softly flows.
In pockets of air so brisk and bright,
They toss about in sheer delight.

The Brush of Fate in Motion

A carousel of colors bright,
They pirouette in pure delight.
Mischief whirls with every gust,
As they dance, it's a must!

They plot and plan their little games,
To tickle feet and call out names.
With every flip and playful spin,
A hearty laugh begins to win.

Beneath the Gathering Storm

A shuffle here, a flap in flight,
Prepare for chaos, what a sight!
They giggle at the coming rain,
As puddles form, they tease the plain.

In swirling winds, they take their stand,
A comedic show, so unplanned.
As thunder rumbles, they just grin,
It's nature's jest, let the fun begin!

Last Call of the Setting Sun

As twilight dances on the ground,
A squirrel prances, joy unbound.
Chasing shadows, making friends,
With goofy leaps that never ends.

The sky blushes in hues of wine,
A raccoon winks, it's dinner time.
With clumsy paws, they tiptoe low,
Stealing snacks and putting on a show.

A turtle plods, just looking lost,
As crickets chirp, they're the boss.
'Hey! I'm late!', the hare declares,
But snores float up from fluffy chairs.

The sun dips low, the moon comes out,
A party starts, without a doubt.
With silly hats and tunes to run,
It's the last call, and oh, what fun!

A Serenade to the Forgotten

In the corner where shadows dwell,
A lone sock starts a tale to tell.
It sways with flair, a dance so bold,
Time forgot it, but it's not old.

Behind the couch, a dust bunny sighs,
With dreams of being a superstar rise.
It gathers crumbs with so much pride,
A fluffy diva, it won't hide.

An old shoe chuckles, cracked and worn,
'The mischief starts where I was born.'
It tells of puddles and muddy days,
Of joyful jumps and crazy plays.

So here's to the knick-knacks, the bits we miss,
In their world, they find pure bliss.
A serenade for the things unseen,
Let's celebrate them, they reign supreme!

Whispers of Autumn's Breath

In the breeze, a tiny hat,
Fallen from a squirrel's chat.
It rolls along the sidewalk's face,
A furry thief in a funny race.

Pumpkin spice in every nook,
A latte sip, then off we look.
A rogue acorn lands with flair,
Bouncing off a shoe with care.

Fragments of a Fading Canopy

Crackling under foot they go,
As kiddos stomp and put on a show.
Each crunching sound a giggle bursts,
Nature's sound effects are the worst!

A gust comes by, what a surprise,
One hat flies up, it reaches the skies!
Like frisbees tossed, they twirl and roll,
Mother Nature takes her toll.

The Dance of Swaying Shadows

Bouncing shadows on the ground,
Playing tag without a sound.
A twirl, a dip, and then a slide,
Who knew the sidewalk was this wide?

Sidewalk chalk, a colorful spree,
Drawing where the grass should be.
With each stroke, a laugh unfolds,
Their smiling faces—brave and bold.

Tattered Pages in the Breeze

A paper plane takes to the sky,
Crafted from a lunch waste pie.
Twirling high, it does a flip,
Waving joy like a playful trip.

Comic strips among the fun,
Spiders giggle in the run.
With every gust, the pages dance,
A funny tale, a quirky chance.

Seasons in the Balance

Spring jumped in wearing bright polka dots,
While winter grumbled, cold and full of snot.
Summer hula-hooped, basking in the sun,
And autumn raised its brow, 'This isn't fun!'

Each season wrestles for the perfect spot,
With snowmen dancing, giving it a shot.
The flowers giggle at the frosty bite,
As they twirl in laughter, what a wild sight!

The Last Glimmer

The evening sun took one last glance,
A final kiss, a cheeky dance.
Clouds plumped up like pillows with flair,
While stars giggled, 'We'll soon be there!'

Moon held a party, with lights so bright,
While crickets crooned in sheer delight.
A firefly slipped, giving a wink,
Lighting up darkness, don't you think?

Whirling in the Twilight

Squirrels in capes twirled through the leaves,
While a wise old owl giggled, 'Oh please!'
Bunnies bounced in their fluffy round shoes,
Dancing in circles, spreading bright blues!

The sun dipped low, a golden balloon,
And twilight chuckled, 'I'll see you soon!'
With comets zooming, the sky played tricks,
Coyote cheered, 'Hey, show me those flicks!'

An Ode to the Fleeting

Time wears a hat, spins fast on its toes,
While moments parade in whimsical clothes.
A tick-tock jester, making us grin,
As we chase each second, let the fun begin!

With laughter aloft in a jolly old dance,
We twirl down the lane, given chance after chance.
The past waves a flag, as the future runs wild,
While the present throws a party, oh what a child!

The Moment Between Graft and Fall

A branch is swaying with style,
Its dance could go on for miles.
With every gust, the laughter flows,
As nature giggles at how it grows.

The fruit is ripe, but oh so vague,
It teases birds, then starts to plague.
Just when you think it's time to munch,
A critter swoops in and steals your lunch!

The colors shift from green to red,
It seems like fashion's gone to bed.
Yet still they dangle, bold and wild,
Like fashion statements gone quite mild.

So here we stand, confused in cheer,
With all this bounty, grab your beer!
The playful fuss of fall's sweet call,
Is just a giggle shared by all.

Murmurs at Twilight's Threshold

The sun dips low, a cheeky grin,
As shadows stretch, the fun begins.
Whispers rustle through the glade,
A chattering chorus, mischief made.

The crickets chirp a silly tune,
While squirrels plot under the moon.
They plan a heist of acorns round,
And giggle softly at the sound.

As twilight creeps, the jokes abound,
A bushy tail, a snicker found.
When shadows waggle, laughter roars,
As night unravels its playful stores.

A chorus hums of quirks and jests,
Just nature's way to pass the tests.
In shimmering dusk, we find our glee,
As twilight's murmurs feel like free.

Shadows of What Once Was

The past is giggling in the breeze,
As shadows stretch with playful ease.
Once grand and proud, now faded slight,
They leap around in silly flight.

The memories wave from tree to tree,
Whispering tales of glee and spree.
But here they dangle, caught in air,
A clumsy bunch without a care.

The echoes bounce on ground and bark,
They tease the night, ignite a spark.
With every rustle, laughter pours,
As history knocks on spirit's doors.

So let's embrace the whimsy bright,
In shades of twilight, pure delight.
For in the whispers of what's past,
We find a joy that's meant to last.

The Path Beneath a Canopy of Change

Underneath the leafy maze,
Lies a path that twists and plays.
With footfalls soft, a dance unplanned,
Each step brings giggles, hand in hand.

Beneath the branches, secrets peek,
A hidden world where giggles speak.
The stones might trip, the roots might tease,
As laughter mingles with the breeze.

In golden hues, the light does bounce,
Creating shadows that seem to pounce.
The ferns perform a lovely jig,
While squirrels clap, oh what a gig!

So skip along this joyful way,
Where laughter echoes, night and day.
For every turn, a surprise awaits,
In the canopy where fun creates.

Soul Dance of the Seasons

In autumn's gown, a squirrel prances,
Chasing hues in silly dances.
With acorns flying, oh what glee!
Nature's jesters, wild and free.

Winter slides with snowy grace,
A penguin's jog, a funny race.
As icebergs wobble and tiptoe,
They laugh and slip in winter's show.

Spring brings bloom and buzzing cheer,
Bees wear jackets, look so dear.
They bump and fumble, all around,
In this wacky nature sound.

Summer waves in its bright attire,
A sunburned crab, caught in the mire.
With flip-flops flapping on seashells,
The season's giggles, loud and swell.

Where the Shadows Play

Beneath the trees, where shadows hide,
A raccoon's snack turns into pride.
Juggling berries with furry grace,
He drops them all, a messy chase.

In twilight's glow, a frog will croak,
Riddles spill from his wispy cloak.
With jokes about flies—a croaker's spree,
His audience? The old oak tree.

The fireflies glow like tiny stars,
Buzzing tales of silly cars.
They zip and zap with glimmer bright,
In a dance-off that lasts all night.

As darkness falls, the laughter's loud,
Creatures gather; they form a crowd.
The moon joins in, a shining face,
To witness their whimsical embrace.

Mementos of Nature's Curtain

A feather drops from a bird's beak,
Lands on a frog who looks quite chic.
They grin and trade a silly glance,
What a pair! They've found romance.

The windy gusts, they tease the trees,
Tickling leaves with playful ease.
Branches dance, they stretch and sway,
Nature's giggle at the end of day.

A wandering rabbit hops in style,
Pausing just to wink and smile.
He tugs on grass, makes silly hats,
Delighted by his own antics—what a brat!

As dusk unfolds its blanket wide,
The critters laugh, no need to hide.
This vibrant show, a grand parade,
Where nature's tricks never fade.

Poised for Release

The butterflies, oh what a sight,
Wrestling flowers for a bite.
In hilarious spins, they whirl and twirl,
A blossoming dance, a floral swirl.

The caterpillars rule the stage,
Dressed in stripes, they act their age.
They wiggle, jiggle, and share their dreams,
A comedy that bursts at the seams.

Chasing clouds, a playful breeze,
Tosses dandelions with such ease.
Seeds fly off like tiny kites,
In a flutter of giggles, pure delights.

As sunset paints the sky in glee,
Nature's jesters—so wild and free.
With each new day, laughter's embrace,
In this bright world, we find our place.

Dancer in the Gale

A twirling leaf took to the sky,
With pirouettes that made me sigh.
It danced around a passing crow,
Who squawked, 'You think you steal the show?'

The wind joined in, a cheeky friend,
Spinning the leaf till it would bend.
It winked at clouds, then did a flip,
'You can't catch me, I'm on a trip!'

Fragments of a Dying Day

As daylight fades, the colors clash,
With oranges bright, and purples flash.
A pile of twigs made a little bed,
While critters laughed at what I said.

Sunsets giggled as shadows grew,
A squirrel plotted what to do.
The sky wore hues, a colorful rack,
Waving goodbye, 'We'll take it back!'

The Final Rustle

A crispy crunch beneath my shoe,
A sneaky trick, a snicker too.
'Is that you, autumn? Playing pranks?'
I jumped a bit, and said my thanks.

The trees shook their branches to tease,
Sending down whispers on the breeze.
A laughter echoed from high above,
Those pesky vines just want our love!

Echoes of the Falling

Every thud and flutter's a jest,
Nature's way of being the best.
Each tumble down is met with cheer,
'Another round, the end is near!'

With every drop, a giggle floats,
A merry dance in leafy coats.
They bounce and roll, they flip and flop,
Saying, 'We'll party, we'll never stop!'

The Edge of Transformation

The wind's a jester, oh what a clown,
Twirling the twigs and painting the town.
With every twist, and each little giggle,
Nature takes stage for a silly wiggle.

Colors explode, like a painter's delight,
Dancing on branches, quite a funny sight.
With crunch in the step, we all join the spree,
As nature's own comedy unfolds with glee!

Drifting Beyond the Trees

A leaf took a tumble, and what did it say?
"I'm just here for laughs, can I stay for the play?"
It rolled with a chuckle, spun under the sun,
Claiming each moment, oh, wasn't it fun?

Squirrels look baffled, loony with cheer,
Chasing their tails, their antics so clear.
As branches do sway, and the world giggles by,
Who knew a small leaf could cause such a sigh?

An Exit in the Breeze

With a tug and a pull, the wind gave a shout,
"Time for a send-off, watch that leaf bounce out!"
It fluttered, it flailed, like a dance out of tune,
Making a dash, in the light of the moon.

Down through the air, it floated and spun,
"Catch me if you can!"—such a whimsical run.
A tumble here, a twirl over there,
Who knew leaving home could be such a dare?

Vignettes of the Changing Sky

The clouds wear expressions both funny and strange,
One looks like a dog—oh, see how it's changed!
As raindrops conspire, they chuckle and play,
Painting funny pictures that brighten the day.

The sun bursts in laughter, shining so bright,
Tickling the leaves with its warm, golden light.
Every shift in the sky offers joy, oh what fun,
As nature spins tales, never to shun!

Carried by the Wind

A tumbleweed rolls with style,
Spinning in circles, a dapper child.
It teases the cats with a cheeky grin,
Saying, 'Catch me if you can!' with a twirl and spin.

The breeze has a laugh, a playful tease,
Whispering secrets through the swaying trees.
A daredevil leaf on a whimsical ride,
Waving goodbye to those left behind.

Remnants of Green

A patch of grass, now not so bright,
Wishes for sunlight, but it's night.
It tells funny tales of a summer dance,
Of bugs in tuxedos and a worm romance.

Dandelions giggle as they float away,
Saying, 'Catch us later, we'll be back someday!'
With roots that shout, 'We're not done here!',
But right now they wave, and disappear.

A Symphony in Decay

Crunchy sounds, a music score,
When a foot falls down, it begs for more.
'Crunch, crunch,' the melody swells,
Out here with nature, who can tell?

The trees hum along with a crackling cheer,
As autumn's orchestra plays somewhere near.
A rusty trumpet, a violin sigh,
Nature's comedy, oh my, oh my!

The Dance of Departure

A twirling leaf on a graceful spree,
Declares it's time for a wild jubilee!
With a spin and a flip, it leaps and whirls,
Sparking laughter, it jigs and twirls.

Across the park, it's quite the show,
Making squirrels laugh as it dips low.
With every little gust, it's the life of the street,
Goodbye, my friends, it's been quite the treat!

When Colors Fade

In autumn's clutches, we all joke,
The trees are laughing, watch them poke.
'Hey, you green one, time to brown!'
Another wardrobe shift goes down.

Crisp and crinkly, what a sight,
Dressed in orange, isn't it bright?
The earth, a canvas gone askew,
Nature's prank? We see right through.

Chasing gusts, they swirl and spin,
Funny how they dance, where to begin?
Gravity says, 'Come on, take flight!',
While squirrels below plan their stuffy night.

Eventually lands, a crunchy sound,
But who's to say what's lost and found?
A pile of giggles, a rustle of cheer,
In the great game of going, we cheer!

Layers of Time

Oh, the layers wrap like a silly gift,
Every season brings its little shift.
Faded green from summer's fuss,
Beware, the colors have much to discuss.

They gather, giggle in a heap,
Remember the days, so wild and deep.
Each shred a story, a playful tease,
Whispering secrets with the breeze.

Time's a layering, brief and quick,
A comical dance, oh what a trick!
They flutter down, as if to say,
'What's wrong with change? It's just play!'

From bright to dull, it's all a game,
Yet every shade is still the same.
In this costume party, what's the crime?
To wear our passage, layer by time.

The Poetry of Parting

With every gust, sighs fill the air,
Funny how the world stops to stare.
A poet's verse, a fluttering line,
As greens bow out to the world divine.

Dramatic exits, it's such a show,
An unexpected turn, mirth in tow.
Farewell dances, take a spin,
Could we get back? Let's try again!

A final twirl, and then they're free,
Floating to the ground, what a spree!
A canvas left, of jokes galore,
Where did that color disappear? Encore!

Their parting gift, a chuckle or two,
'Life's just a joke!' they seem to coo.
In giggling piles, let laughter abound,
As poetry finds its rhythm on the ground.

Echoing Through the Boughs

Listen closely, hear the trees,
Whisper jokes in the nightly breeze.
'Knock, knock!'—who's there, my friend?
It's nature's humor, on it depends.

Echoes dance between the leaves,
Every word a giggle weaves.
Branches sway, their shadows play,
A windy jest—come join the fray!

We trick and tease the setting sun,
A leafy quip unveiled for fun.
As shadows stretch, the giggles grow,
Nature's punchline, don't you know?

So hear the laughter, wild and free,
Through every bough and leafy spree.
A choir of jokes, a rustled cheer,
Life's funny tune is always near!

Cascading Moments

A squirrel took a leap, oh what a sight,
Flipping through the air, a clumsy flight.
Thinking he could dance, he flopped instead,
Landed on his tail, a bit misled.

The autumn breeze tickled a funny itch,
Made the branches sway—oh what a hitch!
A laugh escaped the owl perched nearby,
Said, "You call that acrobatics? Oh, my!"

A chipmunk chuckled, with cheeks full of seeds,
Watching the antics of those in the leads.
Nature's circus unfolds with a giggle here,
Nature's not shy, it wants us to cheer.

With every flutter, a humor so grand,
Whispers a joke from nature's own hand.
Beneath the dancing shadows, we can't help but snicker,
Life's a comedy show, and laughter's the kicker.

A Sigh in the Stillness

In the quiet air, a ponderous pause,
A rabbit sneezed; nature's laughing cause.
The breeze giggled soft, then started to tease,
'Why're you so jumpy? Just enjoy the breeze!'

A butterfly landed, with swagger and flair,
Gave a little twirl, danced without a care.
Its wings flapped wildly, not a clue in the game,
But all of us watching, we felt the same.

The meadow held whispers of secrets obscure,
Bumbles the bee buzzed, a clumsy allure.
He dipped in a flower, then spun like a top,
Trip over his own feet, but wouldn't stop.

In stillness we sighed, at the sight so absurd,
Nature providing her own answered word.
For in moments so funny, our cheers take the stage,
Creating a script on life's vibrant page.

Essence of a Gentle Goodbye

As twilight approached, the sun waved hello,
With a wink, it decided to steal the show.
Clouds dressed in pink, acting all coy,
A slapstick farewell, bursting with joy.

A gust of wind, oh what a spry tease,
Sent hats flying, causing quite the unease.
Neighbors all laughed, chasing their caps,
In this funny breeze, oh how time claps.

The tree bid goodnight, with rustles and shakes,
Its branches a-leaning, for goodness sakes!
A high-flying bird, not ready to quit,
Dropped a feather, hoping to make it a hit.

With each little giggle, the dusk drew near,
In whispers it sang, a tune we could hear.
As stars took their place, in a wink of a light,
Nature's goodbye was a tickle of delight.

Fantasies in Flight

A crow donned a hat, in fanciful styles,
Flew over the park, collecting laughs in piles.
His friends chuckled loudly, hats every hue,
What a wild sight, as they fluttered anew.

The sky played a game, trying out all shades,
With clouds like whipped cream, a sweet masquerade.
As a pigeon appeared with a swagger so slick,
Said, "I'm the king, come watch my cool tricks!"

A wisp of a wind joined in the fun,
Ruffling and tussling 'til the rise of the sun.
The trees gently swayed, adding a groove,
Each branch a dancer, in nature's own move.

In this realm of jest, where giggles take flight,
We embrace the humor wrapped in day's light.
For laughter's the treasure, in whispers so bright,
Where each moment's a fantasy, soaring with delight.

The Message in the Whirlwind

In a whirlwind's dance, oh what a sight,
A sock takes flight, soaring with delight.
It swirls with the winds, doing a twirl,
Chasing laundry dreams in a mad, merry whirl.

Socks unmatched, do they have a plan?
To find cozy feet or start a sock clan?
With every gust, they giggle and glide,
Voting for freedom, they take to the sky!

The broom takes cover, the dust bunnies flee,
As the chaos erupts with glee.
A note flies loose, "Hey, I'm a lost bill!"
It zooms past the cat, giving him a thrill!

So when winds howl, take heed, take care,
Your laundry may plan quite the wild affair.
Embrace the chaos, let joy unhinge,
For in the whirlwind, there's laughter and cringe!

Grace of the Afterglow

When twilight tiptoes in with a grin,
The sky's a canvas, where jokes begin.
Crickets serenade as stars pop out,
While fireflies flicker, casting a shout.

"Hey there, moth, want to join in the light?"
They dance around, a fluttering plight.
But moths are clumsy, and truth be told,
They've got two left wings, and dreams bold!

Grasshoppers hop like they own the show,
Riddled with laughter in the sunset's glow.
"Watch me leap!" one brags with a flurry,
And lands in a puddle — oh, what a hurry!

As darkness settles, we stifle a yawn,
But the night's just starting, come on, come on!
So raise your glass, to silly and bright,
To the grace of these antics, pure delight!

Choreography of the Dying Light

As daylight bows with a comedic flair,
The shadows decide they'll dance in midair.
A chair does the cha-cha, a table twists low,
The cat rolls her eyes, "Oh, do take it slow!"

The sun winks down, "Oh, I'm late, I'm late!"
For a date with the moon to dance at eight.
"Watch my steps!" chirps a bird on the run,
Flaunting her moves, but she's not quite done.

In the corner, a pile of laundry does sway,
To rhythm unique, in disarray.
"Oh, don't mind me, I'm just in a funk,"
Said a sock as it tumbled, a whimsical hunk!

When light bids adieu, and starlight appears,
It's a party of shadows, with silly cheers.
So grab a partner, whoever is near,
In the dance of the dusk, let laughter steer!

Touch of the Whispering Wind

A breeze stirs up, with mischievous glee,
It plays with my hair, it tumbles the leaves.
"Catch me if you can!" it teases and taunts,
As squirrels chase whispers, doing their jaunts.

Among the trees, it starts a grapevine,
"Did you hear what the crow said at lunchtime?"
A rustle here, a giggle there,
As gossip takes flight on the soft gentle air.

But don't get too close, oh no, beware!
For splashes of pollen are floating everywhere!
"Achoo!" goes the rabbit, a sneeze full of cheer,
As the wind chuckles softly, a true puppeteer.

So when the air whispers, don't take it for bland,
Join in the ruckus, come take a stand!
In the tickle of breezes, laughter will soar,
For the world's just a stage, ever wanting more!

The Quiet Fall of Petals

A gentle breeze makes quite a fuss,
Down they go, like a clumsy bus.
They twist and twirl in silly dance,
Waiting for someone to take a chance.

A lowly bug comes rolling by,
Wearing glasses, looking sly.
He stumbles on, then he falls,
Covering the ground like beach ball stalls.

The sunbeam giggles, tickles too,
As petals tumble with a view.
It's a parade of slight chaos,
Who knew nature could be so gloss?

And when the frost turns bright green to brown,
The bugs all wear their tiny frown.
But who could care, it's all a game,
The quiet fall is never the same!

Where the Sky Meets Decay

Up in the realm where the clouds collide,
Strange things happen when none decide.
A banana peel dresses the ground,
Bringing laughter without a sound.

A squirrel tries to catch a snack,
But trips and falls — go, acorn, whack!
The world is giggling at its own mess,
A little chaos can bring some success.

The shadow of a bird flies by,
Whispers secrets in a chirpy sigh.
Moss giggles under its leafy stares,
While ants march forth without any cares.

All around, the colors bleat,
Mixing joy with a twinge of defeat.
As winter peeks with a frosty grin,
I bet it's laughing — let the fun begin!

A Symphony of Shivering Colors

The trees perform a grand charade,
With branches swaying, unafraid.
Mother Nature's the conductor here,
Making laughter ring far and near.

Each hue quivers, a playful shout,
Yet here they are, all jittered out.
Yellow slips on a purple sock,
While orange giggles like a ticking clock.

A chatty breeze decides to play,
Twisting colors in a merry way.
Oh, what a ruckus on every street,
Belly laughs echo beneath their feet.

The final act brings gales of joy,
The trees bow low to the little boy.
Nature's jesters in a brilliant show,
A symphony only colors know!

Fluttering Farewells

Up high the motley mob takes flight,
Bidding adieu with sheer delight.
A twirl, a flip, then a thud!
The ground awaits a leaf's mild bud.

They chatter away as they drift on down,
Like proud old clowns wearing silly brown.
Each one hopes for a landing spree,
On someone's head — oh, can it be?

A gust of wind thinks it's quite the tease,
Tossing them around like playful bees.
With a giggle, they grip and glide,
One last salute before they slide.

Then silence reigns, the stage is set,
With a colorful carpet with no regret.
As the sun dips low, the lights grow dim,
Farewell, dear flyers, on a whim!

The Silent Journey of Time

A squirrel runs past, on a quest,
Chasing a nut, he thinks he's the best.
With acorn in hand, he makes a grand race,
While birds in the trees just chuckle and brace.

The clock on the wall gives a mocking tick,
As leaves dance around, attempting a trick.
Each gust of wind seems to laugh and poke,
At all of us humans, bent under the yoke.

Yet time rolls on, with a slippery grace,
Offering moments, a wild sort of chase.
We trip and we stumble on paths old and new,
But aren't we all just a bit of the zoo?

In every tick-tock, a giggle does grow,
As shadows play tag with the warm summer glow.
So here's to the journey with silly delight,
Where time takes a tumble, oh what a sight!

Treading Softly on Forgotten Trails

A path through the woods, a wiggle and sway,
Where old memories frolic and secretly play.
Each twist of the trail has a joke to unfold,
With laughter wrapped tightly 'round stories of old.

The branches above swing like dancers in tune,
While critters perform under the light of the moon.
A rabbit in sneakers takes giant-sized hops,
As beetles in bow ties sway like little flops.

In echoes of whispers, the shadows do tease,
With giggles that rustle through willowy trees.
Every step feels like tickling the ground,
Where nature and mirth are so tightly wound.

So should you wander and tippy-toe near,
Just know that the path has a ticklish cheer.
With each secret giggle that springs from the air,
Adventure awaits in this whimsical lair!

Portrait of a Rustling Heart

With every flick of green, a heartbeat's tick,
The dance of the dusk plays an old, silly trick.
Each rustle a whisper, a chuckle, a jest,
As trees roll their eyes, fully aware of the fest.

The wind pulls the fabric of silence to tease,
As creatures conspire to tickle the leaves.
A squirrel dons glasses, pretending he's wise,
While worms in their jackets plot world-famous pies.

In the shadowy corners where giggles take flight,
Little whispers of joy take over the night.
Twinkling like stars, they bounce without care,
As hearts join the chorus with laughter to share.

So here's to the humor that nature bestows,
Where tickles and giggles are quite the grand show.
Let the rustling lead us, on adventures so fine,
For life is much sweeter when we laugh in time!

Glimmers of Change in Nature's Palette

In a swirl of colors, a palette of glee,
Where shades of green wiggle in harmony.
The flowers all gossip in hues bright and bold,
As butterflies flutter with stories retold.

When autumn arrives in a flurry of cheer,
The ferns do a tango, it's party time, dear!
A pumpkin in bowler, all round and quite plump,
Dances with apples, they're ready to jump.

The whispers of change bring a grin to the ground,
As grasses have giggles that twirl all around.
Reveling in the chaos of colors that blend,
Nature's great canvas brings laughter, my friend.

So let's toast to the whims of the shifting hues,
To moments of joy that we happily choose.
With each bit of change, a chuckle we gain,
In this wacky world, there's such fun in the rain!

The Edge of What Remains

A squirrel with a hat, so bold and bright,
Dancing through branches, what a sight!
With acorns for shoes, he twirls around,
Laughing at shadows, he leaps from the ground.

A pumpkin on stilts, it wobbles, oh dear!
Spilling its guts, what a silly fear!
The grass is still giggling, the sun seems to wink,
As the critters conspire, and everyone thinks.

A frog sings a tune, croaks go out of style,
While a turtle runs laps, with an awkward smile.
With hats made of daisies, they'll romp and they'll play,
Because the edge of the world is a silly ballet.

In the gleeful chaos, the fun never drifts,
As they share their own quirks, and the best little gifts!
With bubblegum laughter, they cheerfully strut,
All at the edge, where the giggles run amok.

Whirling Memories in the Dawn

In the morning, where snickers collide,
A banana peel slips, oh what a ride!
Chickens in pajamas strut down the lane,
With honks and with clucks, they burst every chain.

A dancing old cat, twirls near a fence,
Both agile and graceful, it makes no sense!
The sun spills its laughter, as it climbs up high,
While the clouds play peekaboo, oh my, oh my!

Rabbits with sunglasses lounge in the grass,
Plotting their escape from the morning's sass.
One jumps and it flips, such a comical sight,
As the whole world giggles, from morning to night.

Rustling and tussling, they frolic in fun,
Creating a ruckus, until the day's done.
With every small joy, and every loud cheep,
In the whirling dawn, it's laughter we reap.

Whispers of Autumn's Breath

A caterpillar crawling, wearing a tie,
Dances with acorns, oh my, oh my!
While pumpkins in bowties sway to the beat,
Raccoons mime whispers, they're just too sweet.

A breeze tells a story, a wink and a ping,
With giggles of squirrels, oh what joy they bring!
A hedgehog named Harold, with quills all afluff,
Looks to the wind, "Is that really enough?"

Bare branches are playing a game of charades,
With each twisting silhouette, the fun never fades.
A parade made of critters, holds banners of cheer,
While shadows applaud, as they draw ever near.

In the rustle of whispers, the stories unwind,
The joy of the silly, the laughter combined.
With autumn's cue, they dance in delight,
As each breath of longing takes flight in the night.

Fragile Farewells

A fence post chortles, 'It's time to move on,'
With starlings in bowties, they sing a new song.
Socks on their heads and giggles in tune,
They bumble and stumble, beneath the full moon.

A goodbye balloon, floats up with a grin,
'Til the pig gives a wave, and the fun will begin.
With sprinkles of laughter, they scatter like dream,
While tumbleweeds tumble—what a wild theme!

The clouds toss confetti, while trees clap their leaves,
As the critters declare, with the heart that believes.
"Each farewell a laugh, and a chance to explore,
When fragile is hearty, it opens the door."

In the midst of goodbyes, they find the best cheer,
As memories linger, and joy is so near.
With a wink and a giggle, they bid world adieu,
On journeys where laughter is always in view.

Chronicles of the Unraveling

In the garden, oh so neat,
A squirrel bounds on tiny feet.
It skitters here, it darts around,
In search of snacks that can be found.

With acorns flying, chips in air,
The antics make me stop and stare.
Old flowers laugh, they twist and bend,
As critters play their games, my friend.

A dandelion, proud and bold,
Wonders how the story's told.
A breeze approaches, whispers sly,
"Time to dance or say goodbye!"

In layers of rust, they huddle tight,
As if they're plotting for a fight.
"What's with the fuss?" a tulip sighs,
"Let's play it cool, no need for cries!"

The wind now joins, a jester's glee,
It tumbles past with wild esprit.
Chasing stories, scattering laughs,
A comedy of nature's crafts.

We watch the show from our front seats,
A carnival of breezy feats.
While mischief blends with colors grand,
We cheer for chaos, hand in hand.

Secrets of the Fading Light

As twilight winks with a golden spark,
The shadows start to play their part.
A chatty firefly glows and beams,
Trying hard to fulfill its dreams.

The sun just giggles, slipping low,
While grasshoppers sing their evening show.
A trio of frogs croaks out a tune,
With raucous notes to welcome moon.

A moth flits by, tipsy and bold,
It thinks that every light is gold.
With a belly flop on a flickering flame,
Hopping back, it feels quite lame.

"Not all that glitters is a paradise,"
The wise old tree creaks with advice.
"Careful there, you'd best take flight,
This humor's best in fading light!"

So laughter echoes in the night,
As creatures dance in loose delight.
The secrets of twilight, wild and bright,
Are best shared with a touch of light.

The Silence of the Gale

When the wind whispers, hold your breath,
A comical rumble of life and death.
The branches wiggle, they twist and bend,
Like they're trying to shake off a friend.

"Oh come now, don't be shy!" they laugh,
"Join us in this swaying staff!
We're all just trees, why take it hard?
Just sing with us and play your card!"

The breeze complains, it's feeling tight,
Wants a silly waltz, a dance tonight.
It tumbles through with a playful spin,
Ruffling feathers on the whimsy wind.

A kite cries out, "Hey, look at me!"
"Caught up in a dance, set me free!"
But the gale chuckles, spins it fast,
"Oh, my dear friend, your time won't last!"

In this silliness, the world's a stage,
With nature's laughter, we engage.
So let us waltz while the gusts do sail,
In the silence of the gale.

Reveries in Hues of Fire

In autumn's glow, the colors burst,
A fiery dance, the leaves rehearsed.
"Let's wine and dine, then twist and shout!"
They tangle up, no doubt about.

The maples boast with scarlet grace,
While whispers flutter at a rapid pace.
They gossip loud of summer's end,
"Who will join us on this trend?"

A pumpkin grins, round and bright,
"Hey, friends, let's party all night!"
With goofy hats and wobbly chairs,
They serve up laughter and costume flairs.

"Do you remember the summer blaze?"
Giggles echo through twilight haze.
"Back when we danced, so carefree and bold,
And didn't worry about the cold?"

Colors swirl in a playful spree,
In reverie of what used to be.
So raise a glass, let's take our cheer,
In hues of fire, find joy, my dear!

Nature's Final Brushstroke

A painter tossed down colors bright,
In every corner, shades take flight.
The trees all giggle, whispering why,
As squirrels parade in a leafy tie.

With every gust, a dance begins,
Each branch below holds tiny sins.
Raccoons roll out in perfect style,
While chipmunks grin, with cheeks worthwhile.

On breezy days, their hats askew,
They jovially play with a shade too blue.
"Who stole the green?" one critter quips,
As birds join in with flapping flips.

In nature's jest, the world turns round,
With laughter echoing all around.
A final brushstroke, what a show!
Where funny pranks and colors flow.

Edge of Dusk's Embrace

At twilight's edge, the shadows creep,
Where giggling friends have gone to sleep.
A grasshopper hops with flair and grace,
While fireflies blink in a dizzy race.

The moon sneaks in with a wink so sly,
Tickling the clouds that float on high.
"Dance with me!" a whisper sings,
As crickets start their evening flings.

A cheeky breeze teases the trees,
"Come have fun, if you please!"
And amid the swirls of dusk's embrace,
A tumbleweed rolls, giving chase.

Laughter spills as shadows twirl,
Each petal sharpens, ready to whirl.
Nightfall comes with playful cheer,
Turning the world into a charming sphere.

Crimson Secrets in the Wind

In whispers bold from branches high,
Crimson secrets flutter by.
Bees giggle with a buzzing sound,
As autumn's mischief spins around.

A crafty crow with hat askew,
Hides shiny treasures in the dew.
"Catch me if you can!" he crows with glee,
While playful winds just set him free.

The tangle of twigs, quite odd and neat,
Turns rustic homes into a treat.
With squirrel chefs atop their stage,
Whipping up feasts of root and sage.

As laughter weaves through branches wide,
The season bursts with vibrant pride.
Crimson secrets dance in tune,
Beneath the watchful golden moon.

The Flight of Fragile Dreams

A butterfly flits, with dreams so bright,
But trips on a breeze, what a funny sight!
He shakes his wings with a goofy grin,
"Let's try that again, oh where to begin?"

Clouds above toss playful jibes,
While daisies laugh, oh how they vibe!
"Come dance with us!" they shout and shout,
"What's life without a little bout?"

With wishes tangled in the air,
The toadstools join, they're unaware.
A playful hop, a gentle swing,
In this wild flight, oh what joy it brings!

As the stars wink in playful jest,
The fragile dreams do their best.
Floating free, what a sweet view,
In the whimsy of the night, all things anew.

Solitary Shimmer

A lone green sprout, quite bold and brave,
Stands tall in a field, a landscape wave.
It winks at the clouds, with a silly grin,
Saying, "Here I am, let the fun begin!"

The ants march by with a fancy dance,
While breezes carry their playful prance.
"Come join my party!" the sprout does shout,
"It's just me and nature, what's life without?"

A butterfly flutters, all decked in hues,
"Is this a garden, or a fashion muse?"
The sprout just laughs, with a twisty jive,
"In the greenery here, we all feel alive!"

The sun takes a peek, pouring gold on the scene,
While the sprout breaks into a dance so serene.
A laugh echoes through this wild frolic,
In the circle of life, it's all so symbolic!

Tapestry of Change

In a world where colors swirl and twine,
I spotted a fellow who seemed benign.
"What's your secret to this joyful spree?"
He shrugged and replied, "Just stay carefree!"

His neighbors giggled, playing hide and seek,
While the wind told tales of the mild and meek.
"Join our fun circus, don't bring a frown,
Here in our patch, we wear joy like a crown!"

A squirrel leaped high, with a nut in tow,
Dropping it squarely, he shouted, "Whoa!"
The sprout just chuckled, unperturbed by the slam,
"Life's just a buffet; please pass the jam!"

Thus together they spin, in a whirl of delight,
No time for worries, just laughter in sight.
As seasons change, the colors will mix,
In this tapestry, we keep finding new tricks!

A Fluttering Soliloquy

A dainty whisper from a branch on high,
Says, "Oh my goodness, I could touch the sky!"
With a bounce and a wiggle, the branch takes a stand,
"Look at me, world! Isn't this just grand?"

Then comes a gust, full of mischief and cheer,
Tickling the branch, with all it holds dear.
"Careful now, wind! Don't ruffle me too!"
Laughter erupts between branches and dew.

A roguish crow joined, with a witty caw,
"You think you're so bright, but I'm the true star!"
"Oh, you want a duel? Let's twirl and spin!"
They danced in a circle, let the games begin!

And if you listen closely, you might hear them laugh,
Crafting a melody of their silly craft.
As dusk softly drapes in a colorful cloak,
They chuckle and twirl; this, no mere joke!

Time's Gentle Caress

Beneath the sun's warm and loving embrace,
A timid sprout tries to find its place.
"Why wait for tomorrow?" it giggles and bends,
"Let's have a party, it's time to make friends!"

With chirping birds and the sun's friendly glow,
The sprout starts a conga line, all in a row.
"Oh come join the fun! Feel the beat of the breeze,
Dance with the shadows, twirl with such ease!"

An old worm chuckles, snuggled in dirt,
He pops up and grins, a bit of a flirt.
"Should I join your line? I'm a slow-moving chap,
But I've got some moves that'll make you all clap!"

So they all come together, a merry brigade,
Spinning and laughing, in this nature parade.
With time gently laughing and flowing so free,
In this joyful moment, they found unity!

The Heart's Last Flutter

A fluttering dance, oh what a sight,
Rushing to land, then taking flight.
In a game of tag with the wind's own breath,
Who knew a leaf could mimic death?

But then it tumbles, a twist and a spin,
A pirouette that would make you grin.
Like a clumsy dancer on a slippery floor,
It chuckles and giggles, then flops once more.

Its companions whisper, 'Is this a joke?'
As it flutters down with a soft-spoken poke.
The heart's last flutter, a comedic spree,
Who knew farewell could be so carefree?

So here's to the clutters in the autumn air,
They laugh at the ground with a joyous flair.
With a final bow from their leafy crew,
They scurry away, all just to amuse you.

A Canvas of Surrender

Colors collide in a clumsy embrace,
As shades lose the battle, they leave not a trace.
Whirls of maroon and bizarre olive green,
Each leaf lets go like it's part of a scene.

A tumble, a roll, down to the street,
Art made from laughter, now that's a treat!
They flutter and flounder, in playful retreat,
Who'd think nature's canvas could be so sweet?

As one slips on down with a raucous cheer,
It lands on a squirrel, who squeaks out in fear.
A tapestry woven with chaotic delight,
In this silly circus, all is just right.

With whispers of humor and chuckles in flight,
They turn the dull pavement into pure light.
So let every fall be a spirited blend,
In the humorous art that the seasons send.

Golden Hues of Passing Time

They drift and they shimmer, these nuggets of cheer,
Falling through time, never living in fear.
Flashing bright colors, it's quite the show,
Who knew the season could dazzle below?

Every gust of wind, every playful shove,
Turns moments to memories, fill them with love.
With giggles they tumble, twirling in play,
Marking the moments just slipping away.

In this carnival whirl, they dance and they spin,
Each pirouette perfect, a cheeky chagrin.
As they settle down, with a glimmering grin,
Who knew the end could look so much like win?

So raise up a toast to the fleeting bright hue,
To moments we treasure, like this little crew.
In the folly of life, they twirl like a mime,
A silly reminder of our golden time.

Patches of Forgotten Dreams

In corners and crevices, they stagger and sway,
Once vibrant with promise, now fading away.
Whispering secrets of the dreams they once held,
In muddy old puddles, their hopes are quite quelled.

A hop and a flop, they scatter about,
Collecting the chuckles from all of the shout.
With patches of laughter and tattered old schemes,
Each idiosyncratic, they float in their dreams.

Each one a character, a tale to unfold,
Once sturdy and bright, now fragile and bold.
As they tango with shadows, shaking off norms,
In a comedic display, like stand-up in storms.

Yet through all this fading, they wink with a jest,
Reminding us all, in our wild, wacky quest:
That even forgotten, there's humor in plight,
In the patches of dreams that dance through the night.

www.ingramcontent.com/pod-product-compliance
Lightning Source LLC
Chambersburg PA
CBHW072217070526
44585CB00015B/1376